Embers among the Ashes
Poems in a Haiku Manner

Charlie R. Braxton

Embers among the Ashes
Poems in a Haiku Manner

Charlie R. Braxton

Introduction by Kalamu ya Salaam

Jawara Press
2017

Other works by Charlie R. Braxton

Ascension from the Ashes (1990)
Gangsta Gumbo (2012)
Cinders Rekindled (2012)

First Printing: 2017

Cover art by Felandus Thames
Photo by Alan T. Harrison
Cover design by Dub G

ISBN-13: 978-0-9836527-1-7

Published in the United States of America by Jawara Press
Charlie.Braxton@gmail.com

Dedication

For Jerry Ward, my mentor, my friend.

Contents

Acknowledgements

In Memory and Wonder:

Mary L. Woodard (Mama), Charlie Braxton, Sr. (Dad), Bonnie Bell Christopher (Mama Bonnie), Elmer Martin (Grandma Elmer), Kemp Braxton (Grandpa Kemp), Maggie Wallace (Grandma Mag), Lillie Braxton Kline (Aunt Lillie), Hugh Earl Braxton, Sr., Marie Braxton (Aunt Marie), June Woodard, Mrs. Geneva Woodard, J.L. Woodard, Mary (Maggie) Magee, L.J. Martin, Leola Martin, Joe Martin, Jerry Martin, Phillip Martin, Larry Martin, Virgie Brock-Shedd, Nayo-Barbara Watkins, Jean Chamberlain, Richard Wright, Warring Cunney, George Kent, Saint Claire Bourne, Etheridge Knight, Ted Joans, Langston Hughes, Margaret Walker Alexander, Rosa Lee Daniels, Tom Dent, Gwendolyn Brooks, Martin Luther King, Jr., Malcolm X, Amiri Baraka, Mari Evans, Bob Kaufman, Dudley Randle, Jayne Cortez, Harold Cruse, Frances Cress-Welsing, Amos Wilson, Gil Scott-Heron, Jimi Hendrix, Bo Diddley, Larry Neal, Henry Dumas, Josef Ben-Jochannan, Ebon Dooley, L.C. Dorsey, Willie Cook, Bob Marley, Peter Tosh, Mikey Smith, Marvin Gaye, Sam Cooke, Larry Neal, Otis Redding, Peter Tosh, Mikey Smith, Isaac Hayes, James Brown, Howling Wolf, B.B. King, Robert Johnson, Muddy Waters, John Coltrane, Miles Davis, Kwame Toure, Kwame Nkrumah, Amilcar Cabral, Fela, Tupac Amaru Shakur, Ivan Van Sertima, Asa Hilliard, Aime Cesaire, Franz Fanon, Loraine Hansberry, Leopold Shengor, Chokwe Lumumba, Patrice Lumumba, Cheikh Anta Diop and countless others who inspired me to express myself with words.

In Appreciation and Honor:

Johnnie Robinson, Calvin Braxton, Kwame Braxton, Hope Robinson, Kamau Braxton, Nzinga Braxton, Nile Braxton, Keri Robinson, Kamiyah Braxton, Kristian Braxton and Inaayah Braxton, Kimberly Braxton-Brown, Calvin Kees, Charlie Braxton (brother).

Jerry Ward, Kalamu ya Salaam, Askia M. Toure, Ishmael Reed, Al Young, Sonia Sanchez, Haki R. Madhubuti, Sterling D. Plumpp, Jolivette Anderson-Douoning, Eugene B. Redmond, Nikki Giovanni, Nikki Finney, Tony Medina, Tony Bolden, Quincy Troupe, Nia Damali, Akbar Imhotep, Pearl Cleage, Shay Love, E. Ethelbert Miller, Lenard D. Moore, Rufus Mapp, Greg Jackson, Mariba Lumumba, Curtis Austin, Warren Gilmore, Barrett Pickett, Jarl Tobias, Nettie Stowers, Ira Sullivan, Kevin Powell, Kamau Daud, Kimberly Collins, Asha Bandele, Saul Williams, Mos Def, J. Cole, Big KRIT, Outkast, Michael Gonzalas, Muhammad ben Abdallah, Sandra Shattuck, Allen Gordon, Darryl Pete, Richard Jones, Mia X, Dominique D'Leo, Noel Didla, Carlotta Abrams, Brian Lassiter, Donnie Cross, Eric Robinson, Jean-Pierre Labarthe, Oku Onura, Felandus Thames, C. Liegh McInnis, Teresa N. Washington, Jocelyn Wilson, Regina Bradley, Maco Faniel, Milton Nacimento, Gilberto Gil, Jorge Ben, Carlton Wade, Langston Collins, Mark Anthony-Neal, Chuck D, Brother J, Rakim, George Clinton, Kiese Laymon, Goodie Mob, Tommy "T-Bone" Pruitt, Michael Renders, Tiffany Austin, helen crump and, of course, countless others who struggle with me to write a better world.

Introduction

LOOK. SEE. SEEN.

The haiku is a traditional Japanese poetry form. In English literature the emphasis is usually on the layout: three lines, five syllables in the first and third lines and seven syllables in the second line. There is often a nature image employed. Although that is the formality, there is, of course, much more to the successful use of haiku.

Some of us black poets have been attempting to fit in and/or extend haiku in the context of African-American literature, i.e. we are not simply writing nature poems, we write from a liberation perspective both in terms of content and aesthetics. Our content is often unabashedly in opposition to oppression, and our aesthetics emphasizes musical elements and improvisation (by playing with form, sometimes in very unconventional ways).

Within the context of innovation we point to the three phases of haiku writing.

Phase one is the pointing finger that instructs us to "look" at such and such. In this case the poem is a signpost pointing us towards whatever it is the poet wishes the audience to "see" (i.e. regard, consider, understand, feel).

Phase two is to accurately describe or depict that which is to be regarded, and to do so succinctly, i.e. with a minimum of words. In this case the goal is to be as specific as possible in terms of what is shown in an extremely brief format.

Phase three is to give the import or impact, or to replicate the experience itself, and hopefully illuminate the meaning. Some poets believe that if the import or impact is expertly done then there is no need to spell out the experience or the meaning as those qualities will be obvious. Others believe that the deepest meaning is often hidden in plain sight and that most people need a guide to help them discern even that which is obvious.

How-so-ever the poet chooses to undertake the poetic expression, emphasizing whichever phase or combination of phases – that is where the poetry is found. Not simply in the thing itself but in how well, how effectively the thing is presented, whether it is an admonition to look, a picture of what we wish our audience to behold, or the often most difficult undertaking of sharing an experience/sensation or sharing an understanding/viewpoint. This is our task as poets.

Everyone who reads or hears the poem is a critic in the sense that they either get it or don't get it depending both on how well the poet does the job of poeting, and how sensitive is the audience in responding to the poetry. The professional critic, of course, undertakes to contextualize the poem and to explicate how well or how accurately the poem fulfills its mission.

Some people argue that the poet writes best about what the poet knows firsthand, others believe that the craft of poetry supersedes reportage and memoir, that the poem does not have to be true, i.e. factual, to the poet to ultimately work but rather true to the subject matter. Authenticity, or sticking only to the facts, is not a simple question. While the folk saying is often true that who feels it knows it, it is also true that we often need guides to tell us what it is we are experiencing and/or to share with us feelings and understanding that are personally foreign but humanly relevant.

I will conclude this short introduction to the haiku of Charlie Braxton with what amounts to a particularly striking haiku-like image: "see the girl with the red dress on / she can birdland all night long, oh yeah!". There is so much happening in that short phrase popularized by Ray Charles. The meaning of the line is obvious on one level but also multifaceted in its cultural and sensual implications.

Most listeners are so struck by the image that they never stop to consider that Ray Charles is blind. He can not see the girl even though he is telling us to look at her and we all see her. How is it possible that we the audience are led to see a sight the poet physically can not see? Ah, that is the magic of poetry. We poets, blind though we may be, we will gift you with visions.

We will help you look at life, see life in its many permutations, and gain both a feel for and an understanding of life. Look at what Charlie has to say, consider the visions he shares, feel and understand the deep blues, the exultant reds, and the profound gold of touching and being touched by a deeper appreciation of life.

Kalamu ya Salaam
New Orleans, July 2016

Art is the illusion of spontaneity.

--Japanese Proverb

One good thing about music: when it hits, you feel no pain.
-Bob Marley

SECTION ONE

Blues for B.B.

black boy bellows pain
throughout the streets of memphis,
blues stay on my mind.

mississippi roads
sing songs of sorrow seeing
its son says *so long*

Fire House Rhythm Rock

fire house rhythm
jam dubplate as we skank 'pon de
beat, root rock reggae.

african herbsman
hustling culture vibes and free-
dom from white jesus

on this day we say
we want an african god
as black as the night

dub 'pon de rock rid-
dim a shake and a shake, na
break black root's foundation

Embers among the Ashes

Musing on the Blues

magnolia blues
blooms with mississippi pain,
black & miserable

the scars scratched on her
black back extract cotton from
earth salted with tears

blood runs down river
cawing crows echo cries of
melancholy moans

hushed tones of my
native tongue spoken in dark-
ness, wait for response

they brought us here to
work but nobody hired us
nor have we been paid

For Louis Johnson

thunder thumbs left lighten-
ing licks riding a rocket
straight to ogun's arms

Charlie R. Braxton

Winter Blues: Chi-town

the winters up north
are as cold and brutal as
a mean southern boss.

the wind laughing at
the broke furnace on the wall-
sounds like landlord's voice.

the owner of the
corner store is as rotten
as the meat he sells.

these chicago streets
are cold, hard, wet and grey, ain't
nobody's gold here.

a puff of smoke, a
swig of wine may pass the time
still won't ease my mind.

she said she was tired
of living life hand to mouth
can do that down south

Embers among the Ashes

For Ornette Coleman

who will stoke the coals
now that colossus is gone?
who will keep the code?

who among us will
keep the home fire lit amidst
the big bland wet mist?

who will play our tunes
belt our blues, chant our black psalms
in the darkest night?

who will sing our songs,
tell us our his/story when
all is forgotten?

who will remind us
now that ornette's long gone?
who will do it, who?

The March

birmingham sings the
blues while edmond pettus bleeds
sunday's gospel truth

Forrest Folk Blues

a lizard lounges
on a lily pad, relaxing
like a cat, all cool

crickets croon the tunes
while cicadas sling notes, folk
blues for the forest

For Saint John the Coltrane

saxophone solo
jaunting through my mind reminds
me of grand old saints

singing and playing
variations of blues, wea-
ry, ancient and black

arpeggio notes
crescendo into sheets on
sheets of solid sound

sailing on a ship
made of shango's iron, float-
ing on oya's blue sea

Embers among the Ashes

The Gospel According to James Brown

rhythm rips through me
like holy ghost on Sunday
morning, I feel good!

Azul

sunset blues song sings
sullen sorrow as tears rain
in new tomorrows

Brazilian Blues

bossa nova blues
beat breaks through silent night like
light cuts through darkness

bahia, my love
longs for you like a summer
day pines for cool nights

Goddess from Bahia

favela girl walks
the streets of bahia her
hips sway like samba

and the sweet pitter
patter of her feet beat out
bossa nova tunes

her cinnamon breasts
the size of ripe cantaloupe
that taste just as sweet

in our true homeland
she would be a queen maiden.
here she's just a maid.

she gave birth to the
nation's culture, nurtured it
with her big *bunda.*

they only see her
as nothing more than the help.
we see her as god.

Embers among the Ashes

For Chuck D

may all your words be
bullets of black thought and your
uzi weigh a ton.

Sax Man Wailing

he enters the stage
horn in hand, mic on stand with
iron lungs blowing.

red rings rolling sparks
off his ivory axe, blue
notes run through the past.

ear drums bleeding black
beats, ancient, ancestral sounds
sing songs of sorrow.

saxophone solo
jaunting through my mind reminds
me of grand old saints

singing and playing
variations of blues, wea-
ry, ancient and black

Melody Sails

and you can sing me
the song of a thousand notes
in sweet lush tones

an arpeggio
of blue notes floating on a
sea of broken reeds

the melody sails
on/off into the hori-
zon, seeking sunset

Transitions
(for Maurice White)

body given to
earth, soul flowing with the wind
spirits burn anew.

when ashes turn to
dust and flesh returns to earth
spirits rise like smoke.

more recently, the
fire in your eyes faded
yet the light shines on.

What about this
over-crowded land
How much more abuse from
man can she stand?
-Marvin Gaye

SECTION TWO

Natural Musings

1.
blue moon river flows
with sparkling water crystal
clear, calm, cool and sweet

2.
lotus blossoms bloom
bringing sweet nectar to life
& gets my bees buzzing

3.
night crawls across the
evening sky bringing darkness
like clouds bring dense rain

4.
black sand beach, white foam
on blue water, yellow sun
reflects off wet rocks

5.
clouds creep across the
indigo sky like shadows
try to dodge the sun

6.
dirt delta black, grass
savannah green, sky ocean
blue, colors of earth

Embers among the Ashes

7.
bodies committed
to soil as spirits commune
with the universe

8.
dust rises like bak-
er's heat in the middle of
may. summer's so here

9.
sunset sunlight peers
through cracked gates of gold as smoke
fades into evening

10.
onyx skies re-
flect light kisses from fire
flies in a glass jar

11.
lightning bug lives in
a glass prison, hope remains
rich -rays reach skyward

12.
smoke dances on wa-
ter as fire clings to ice,
the two curse the night

13.
stars are the eyes of
night, peering through the darkness
deep into your soul

14.
cawing crows soar through
azure skies, cottony
clouds caress their wings

15.
bright white stars pierce through
the blackened sky their sparkle
lighting up the night

16.
skinny trees stripped of
leaves, its lithe limbs shaking
in the autumn breeze

17.
sea water dances
its way to the shoreline, its
tides tide to the moon

18.
torch to grass, flame to
earth, smoke rising, black ashes
floating on the wind

Embers among the Ashes

19.
sun climbs horizon
a black spider scampering
across a blue wall

20.
tsunami winds bring
ocean spray, the mist hides tears
of a tragic night

21.
dark black sky is the
color of gods, their sharp eyes
watching over us

22.
the hills have eyes wild
as a thousand nights tucked un-
der african stars

23.
under the cano-
py of darkness & twink-
ling lights we found god

24.
emerging from the
loving loam of god's garden
comes humanity

Charlie R. Braxton

Spring Blossoms

'nolia blossoms
brightly bloom as humming birds
slowly suck sweet sap

Of Water and Justice
(*for Kamiyah, Keri and Kristian*)

lone acts done in the
name of justice can be like
rocks tossed in water

a small pebble can
make lots of waves in water,
inspire tides at sea

Katrina

god was willing but
didn't stop the water's rise
when the levees broke

Embers among the Ashes

The Spirit of New Orleans

when the hurricane
came, we survived, levees broke
and we are still here

Deep in the Valley

evening rests on the
shoulders of night, waiting on
darkness to come on

way down deep in the
valleys of Mississippi
change waits like a hawk

a new day breaks when
evil scatters in the face
of the morning sun

Inhale

the real zest of life
is hidden deep within the
breath of life. Inhale.

Charlie R. Braxton

Transitions II
(for Claude McInnis & Thelma Lawrence)

earthen flesh returns
to dust, life gone, spirits rise
like light, travels on

Inaayah

black nova explodes
light burst spread out, sparks fall down
deep into the night

Earth Mother
(for Mut Asheru)

mut, so blue your sky
with fluffy clouds floating by
you smile and sun shines

you weep and rain falls
floods the earth with water flow-
ing from the river

hail, goddess mother
give/her of all light & life
calf we know as earth

Why, why, tell 'em that it's human nature.
-Michael Jackson

SECTION THREE

Charlie R. Braxton

The Hidden History of Rice

in paddies of rice,
we toiled, knees bent, head bowed, feet
steeped in rich black mud

sun up, sun down we
stooped, shitting in watery
fields of raw white rice

ole mean missy loved
her some rice puddin', too bad
it didn't love her

be mindful of the
rice you eat, each grain might be
tainted with poison

Question on War

why must poor people
always die en masse making
money for the rich?

Embers among the Ashes

Flint

an assault on both
our houses bring plagues wrought by
instruments of death.

water, elixir
of life, sweet liquid of god-
sabotaged by greed.

Ferguson

darkness on inner
city streets brings blue terror
blood spills on concrete

far too many moans
and bitter tears sully streets...
tired of this shit

B'more, O' B'more

light reflecting from
spring moon shines on city street
bad omen for peace.

baltimore streets are
plenty restless like lions
on a bare stomach.

tear gas smoke rises
like morning fog choking a
child seeking justice.

Ghetto Bird

ghetto bird roams the
urban skyline dropping light
beams looking for prey

Code Switching

to avoid gringo's
ears when he's near I habla
no english, comprende!

Embers among the Ashes

Riot

the faraway look
in your eyes, the fire in your
belly says it's time!

through the thick choking
mist of gas rises a closed
black fist, defiant

there's only so much
a person can take when their
all has been given

After the Riots

among the ashes
embers glow white hot, hope's spark-
ling in the dark holes

Brutus Says...

render unto cea-
sar that which is his justice
then swiftly kill him

Charlie R. Braxton

Yellow Rain
(for Prince Rogers Nelson)

chemical seed placed
in the clouds causes the sky
to cry death to earth.

Notes on the Country Club Crew

'though they make it look
so simple, it can't be ea-
sy oppressing folk

know, the sudden pain
felt in your gut is not a
knife. It is your fear.

The Question Is

if life is precious
then why is death so common
and so goddamn cheap?

Embers among the Ashes

Truth Is

somewhere between nuts
and evil are the lies
of capitalism

the poor are born a-
gainst the wishes of the rich &
live against their odds.

The Zombies of Wall Street

scabs from the sores of
the poor become feast for the
zombies of wall street

money may make a
zombie look good but they still
smell like rotten flesh

Note to Modern Day Uncle Toms

die: what uncle toms
should do when cooning is no
longer required.

Loku for Coon-Ass Authors

self-hating negro
with a pen is like monkey
with a straight razor

Das Spiel: Election Cycle 2016

broken bottles on
empty streets/ politicians
speak of empty hope/

and we believe in
the spin/ the dream/world wide web
of sweet words/ that lie

when statesmen dance/ to
songs only a devil can
hear /things have gone bad

Embers among the Ashes

Desert Storm

    'nother day comes
                               a river of dust rises sol-
diers march onward

clear day, calm sky, no
        obstructing clouds. the iron
                bird shits death like rain.

           hell is a place on
earth called war where bullets fly
               like burning brimstone

when blowback from your
           iron hawk returns do know
your war means our blood

Fall and Decline

rome burned, as nero
fiddled, smoke gets in his eyes
yet he sheds no tears.

these kings are crazy,
their ill minds crazed with the dark-
ness of lust and greed.

who will save their souls
when all the city burns, its
ashes turn to dust?

Dark Roads

dark roads sing gothic
blues through the tightened throats of
spooks whose souls still hang.

deep in the midst of
southern cotton fields, tension
mounts blood boils over.

the howling wolves sound
echo against the bark of
trees. dark times a come.

Embers among the Ashes

Armageddon

a red devil moon
rises over grey flannel
sky. hail falls like rocks.

rocks turn to brimstone,
oceans boiling dry, crops die
like a poisoned fly.

some say these are signs
of the last days coming, that
god is through with us.

and well he should be.
we have done god no favors...
raping our mother.

Limping Simba

the imperial
lion limps along looking
for his own sunset.

there are no horses
here in briton and all the
mules are too stubborn

Southern Soul

down here in the south
the soil is so rich, so deep
so strong and so black

we wage war with our
music our souls prostrate to
god, black fist in air

and we will not be
moved by all the sour notes of
your disharmony

Neo-liberal Logic

look at the fat cats
holding on to their fat sacks
tell the poor get back

the rich keep telling
us that all will be well as
long as they get paid

doesn't matter how
good rich rhetoric sounds, the
wealth never comes

Embers among the Ashes

Port of London

london fog lingers
low, a thick lull lies about
the ship's dark cargo

Broken

the eagle flies in-
to the sun on broken wings
made with blood-soaked gauze

Desert Storm II

dust devil's tail whirls
in the desert wind, here oil
is thicker than blood

water washes sand
and blood from the scarred bod-
ies of dead soldiers

For She Who Rules the Seas Seven

brazilian sun sets
behind the rhythmic ocean
the waves bathe her hips

water glistening
off curls in her hair prompt im-
ages of crown jewels

the light from the gems
in her diadem shines bright-
er than a nimbus

somewhere along the
shoreline devotees dance to
the holy drumbeat

wet sand beneath their
feet is the savory salt
of sacred water

candles lit in the
western wind set sail in the
ocean headed east

aquatic queen of
the seven seas take me back
to the land i love

Embers among the Ashes

To Be Read on Confederate History Month

when the war was ov-
er johnny reb came home whist-
ling lies to dixie

if you listen to
the vile lies of dixie the
south will never rise

One-way Ticket

when the check is cut
uncle ben boards the coon train
and rides all night long

A Dialogue on the Absurdity of Race

curly, the white guy
told me, "fair skin blacks got some
white in their bloodline."

i replied, the curls
in his hair means somewhere there's

African in his.

The Harsh Truth

the greedy drink from
goblets of gold while the poor
have nothing to drink

when their dogs eat bet
-ter than the poor then the soul
of the rich is sick

the land they live on
is always gated and locked
their house is a cage

Play-dough's Fools

burrowed deep beneath
the mountain lie dark caves where
giant shadows dance

nestled in gloomy
caves a gang of fools gather
by fire, searching

heat from the flame warms
their bones and cast shadows that
fools see as monsters

Embers among the Ashes

Appalled at Mississippi (*for Phil Bryant*)

a persistent pall
of heinous hate hangs over
our mississippi

the land where the ghost
of unsolved murders roam free
as rabid dogs howl,

crickets chirp, minor
birds sing the bitter blues fused
with a shocking pain

"america can
do what it wants but this right
here is god's country"

even though it seems
god has abandoned us some
long, long time ago

left us for safer
places with saner people
where love lives freely

Charlie R. Braxton

Cubana Girl

eyes, the color
of rum & coke, her skin, rich & smooth
as ground cinnamon

she speaks no english
i no espanol, mu-
sic starts & we are one

the rhythms of the tom
tom play cha cha cha throughout
the wild, wild night

warm nights swinging in
old havana, her hips rock
to a rumba beat

Only

in mississippi
the black snake moans because he
knows that white cats kill

Embers among the Ashes

Middle Passage

amidst the din of
foreign chatter and stench, i
swallow pain and fear

iron chains may bind
my flesh but it will never
capture my spirit

at night sweet dreams of
home soothes my troubled soul 'til
the bile wakes me up

Money Changers

jesus came back to
the world, whip in hand, headed
down wall street, mad.

Afterword

This book is the culmination of a yearlong exercise in poetic discipline. It grew organically out of an experiment Jerry Ward initiated via a challenge to various poets. The challenge was for poets to write one haiku and one kwansaba on alternate days for a full month. I was one of those poets who accepted the challenge. I did so primarily because I wanted to challenge myself as a poet. I wanted to see if I could complete the challenge. I had read somewhere that Richard Wright wrote at least one haiku a day. I figured that if Richard Wright could write a haiku on a daily basis for years, then surely I could write them every other day for a month. Not that I feel that I can match Wright's exemplary investment; in fact, that would be impossible. But I was willing to give it the old college try. After the 30 days, I became so enamored with the form that I kept on writing. I wrote at least one haiku a day for a solid year. What I gleaned from Wright's example is how incredibly disciplined one must be to write haiku on a consistent basis. It, to borrow the words of the late, great Mississippi poet, Etheridge Knight, "ain't no square poet's job."

After reading this book, those of you who are avid readers of haiku will notice that the poems in this book are not typical of the haiku form. While all of the poems fit the traditional American structural format of five-seven-five syllables per line, they do not always contain references to nature per se'. Quite frankly, I find writing poetry that concentrates solely on nature in the traditional "art-for-art sake" mode to be boring. Haiku which do omit nature references and openly deal with social issues belong to a different strand of poetry. It is poetry where nature is referenced in the broader sense of the word. And that reference is human nature, the peculiar way we, as human beings, treat or mistreat each other based on superficialities that have absolutely nothing to do with whether or not we are decent human beings. Many of the poems refrain from including a *kigo,* an allusion to the season. Some of the poems use simile, another no-no in traditional haiku. As I have said before, these are not your traditional haiku, nor was it ever meant to be.

By using the haiku form to examine themes of how history connects to the current human condition, more specifically how history connects to the current conditions that people of African descent as well as others are experiencing, I am (along with other poets who choose to write in this vein) consciously engaging in what critic, Jerry Ward calls Abrasive Remembering. According to Ward, Abrasive Remembering is "the space where language gives birth to images of an iconic moment in America's violent past. These morph into kindred images of a terrible present."[1] By connecting the "violent past" to the "terrible present," it is my goal to illustrate how the intersectionality of past and present evils form a pattern of negative and exploitive human behavior that we, as humans, must not allow to exist in our children's and our grandchildren's future.

Charlie R. Braxton
Jackson, Mississippi, April 2017

[1] Ward, Jerry (Friday, January 1, 2016), Emmitt Till, Poetry and History, [Blogpost] Retrieved on April 16, 2017 at http://jerryward.blogspot.com/2016/01/emmett-till-poetry-and-history.html.

See also Ward's "Abrasion: Aesthetic Challenges in African American Poetry." *Journal of Ethnic American Literature*, Issue 5 (2015): 22-34.

www.ingramcontent.com/pod-product-compliance
Lightning Source LLC
Chambersburg PA
CBHW032034090426
42741CB00006B/815